FROM A CELL TO SOCIETY

"A REINTEGRATION HANDBOOK"

DeJuan L. Verrett

FROM A CELL TO SOCIETY

"A REINTEGRATION HANDBOOK"
Written By
DeJuan L. Verrett

Disclaimer for From a Cell to Society: A Reintegration Handbook

From a Cell to Society: A Reintegration Handbook" is intended to provide general information and guidance regarding the reintegration process for ex-felons and their loved ones. The information contained in this handbook is not intended as legal, financial, or professional advice and should not be relied upon as such. The author and publisher do not assume any liability for any errors or omissions or for any actions taken in reliance on the information contained in this handbook. It is important to consult with a qualified professional for specific advice tailored to your individual circumstances. The information contained in this handbook may be subject to change and is not guaranteed to be complete or up-to-date. This handbook is not intended to be a one-size-fits-all guide, but rather a resource to help individuals and families navigate the process and build a better future.

Table of Contents

DEDICATION

To all of the formerly incarcerated individuals who have had to navigate the complex and often-difficult process of reintegration into society, we offer our sincerest admiration and respect. I recognize that this process is not easy, and that it is often accompanied by a wide range of challenges and obstacles. Despite these challenges, you have continued to persevere, to strive for a better future, and to make a positive impact in your communities.

I hope that this book will serve as a helpful resource as you navigate the reintegration process, and that it will provide you with the tools, support, and guidance you need to build a fulfilling and successful life after prison. We also hope that it will serve as a reminder that you are not alone in this journey, and that there are many people and resources available to support you along the way.

To the families and loved ones of the formerly incarcerated, we extend our gratitude and appreciation for the vital role you play in supporting and advocating for your loved ones during this challenging time. Your love, support, and understanding are invaluable, and they make all the difference in helping your loved ones to succeed and thrive.

I hope that this book will be a source of hope, inspiration, and guidance for all who read it, and that it will help to support and empower those who are working to build a brighter future for themselves and their communities.

Thank you!
DeJuan L. Verrett

ACKNOWLEDGEMENTS

I would like to extend my heartfelt gratitude and appreciation to all of the individuals who have inspired me to the creation of this book. Your insights, expertise, has been invaluable in helping me to create a comprehensive and helpful resource for the formerly incarcerated and their families.

I want to especially acknowledge the incarcerated individuals who generously shared their stories and experiences with us. The honesty, and vulnerability, has inspired me, and we hope that this handbook will empower others who are navigating the reintegration process.

We at Urban Community Action Network, Inc would also like to thank the family members and loved ones of the formerly incarcerated who have supported and contributed to Urban Community Action Network, Inc., and this project. Your insights and perspectives have added depth and understanding to this book, and we are grateful for your willingness to share your experiences with us.

Remember, together we can make a difference.

Forward By
Seth Ferranti

Seth Ferranti is a filmmaker and journalist who served 21 years in federal prison for a non-violent LSD/cannabis offense.

I am pleased to present this handbook, which is   to provide guidance, support, and resources to individuals who are navigating the challenges of reintegration into society. The reintegration process can be difficult and complex, and it requires resilience, determination, and a strong support network. This book is intended to serve as a helpful resource for those who are facing these challenges, and to provide them with the tools and knowledge they need to succeed.

The chapters in this book cover a wide range of topics that are important for the reintegration process, including understanding the challenges of reintegration, building a strong support network, managing finances and finding employment, navigating the legal system, addressing mental health and substance abuse, practicing self-care, building and maintaining positive relationships, creating a plan for the future, finding housing and building a home, and connecting with community resources.

I hope that this book will provide a valuable resource for all who read it, and that it will empower and support those who are working to build a better future for themselves and their communities. I believe that with the right knowledge, resources, and support, anyone can overcome the challenges of reintegration and build a fulfilling and successful life after prison.

ABOUT THE AUTHOR

De'Juan "DJ" Verrett's journey from a life in prison to an amazing life is truly inspiring. On February 6, 1990, at the age of 19, DJ was arrested on drug charges and sentenced to 20 years in prison. Despite the challenges and setbacks, he faced during his time in prison, DJ never lost sight of his potential and his desire to turn his life around.

After serving 17 years in some of America's most notorious federal prisons, DJ was released in 2007. Rather than dwelling on his past mistakes, DJ used his experiences to fuel his determination to make a positive change in his life. He dedicated himself to personal growth and self-improvement, and worked tirelessly to turn his life around.

Today, DJ's message of self-discovery and positive change is not only thought-provoking, it is powerful and compelling. He has inspired countless people with his story of resilience and determination, and has proven that no matter how difficult the journey may seem, it is always possible to turn your life around and achieve your dreams. DJ's story is a testament to the strength of the human spirit and the power of personal transformation.

This inspiring journey led to the creation of DJ's Los Angeles-based 501(c)(3) nonprofit organization, the Urban Community Action Network, Inc. (U.C.A.N). Founded in 2018, U.C.A.N is dedicated to helping individuals and families in underserved urban communities overcome the challenges they face and reach their full potential. Through programs and services focused on education, employment, and personal development, U.C.A.N empowers individuals to take control of their lives and create a brighter future for themselves and their families.

In the years since its founding, U.C.A.N has made a significant impact in the Los Angeles community.
Its programs have helped thousands of individuals and families improve their lives and achieve their goals, and it has become a vital resource for those in need.

If you would like to learn more about U.C.A.N and support their efforts, please visit their website at **www.ucanla.org.** Whether through financial contributions, volunteering your time, or simply spreading the word about
the important work they do, there are many ways to get involved and make a difference.

INTRODUCTION

Welcome to "From a Cell to Society: *A Reintegration Handbook*"!

If you or a loved one has recently been released from prison, you may be feeling a mix of emotions: excitement, nervousness, and perhaps even fear about what the future holds. The reintegration process can be challenging, but it is also an opportunity for growth and a chance to build a better future for yourself and your loved ones.

This handbook has been created by a former ex-felon (*the author of this book*) to provide guidance and support for ex-felons as you navigate the challenges of reintegration. It includes chapters on building a support system, managing finances, finding employment, navigating the legal system, addressing mental health and substance abuse, and more.

I understand that every person's journey is unique, and that the reintegration process will look different for everyone. This handbook is not meant to be a one-size-fits-all guide, but rather a resource to help you find the tools and support you need to succeed.

I also recognize that the reintegration process can be difficult not just for the ex-felon, but also for their loved ones. If you are a family member or friend of someone who has been released from prison, this handbook can also provide you with information and resources to support your loved one as they navigate the challenges of reintegration.

I hope that this handbook will serve as a helpful resource as you work towards building a better future for yourself and your loved ones. Remember, you are not alone in this journey, and there are people and resources available to help you succeed. Don't be afraid to reach out for support when you need it.

Best wishes for a successful reintegration.

Chapter 1: Understanding the Challenges of Reintegration

Reintegration can be a challenging process, but it is also an opportunity for growth and a chance to build a better future for yourself. In this chapter, we will discuss some of the challenges you may face as you reintegrate into society, and provide strategies for overcoming these challenges.

Adjusting to life outside of prison: After being incarcerated, adjusting to life outside of prison can be difficult. You may have to get used to a new routine, new surroundings, and new social dynamics. It can be helpful to take things one step at a time and give yourself time to adjust.

Here are some additional tips for adjusting to life outside of prison:

Take things one step at a time: It can be overwhelming to adjust to life outside of prison, so it can be helpful to take things one step at a time. Focus on one task or goal at a time, and don't be too hard on yourself if things don't go as planned. Remember, you have been through a lot, and it is important to be kind to yourself as you adjust to your new surroundings.

Seek out support and resources: There are many resources available to help you adjust to life outside of prison. This may include support groups, counseling services, or community resources. It can be helpful to connect with others who have experienced similar challenges and to seek out guidance and support from people who understand what you are going through. Don't be afraid to reach out for help when you need it.

Find healthy ways to cope with stress: Adjusting to life outside of prison can be stressful, so it is important to find healthy ways to cope with stress. This may include exercise, meditation, or talking to a trusted friend or loved one. It may also be helpful to set aside time for activities that you enjoy, such as hobbies or spending time with loved ones.

Build a routine: Establishing a routine can help you feel more grounded and in control of your life. This may include setting regular wake-up times, meal times, and bedtimes, as well as setting aside time for activities you enjoy. Having a routine can provide a sense of structure and stability, which can be especially important during times of transition.

Stay connected with loved ones: Building and maintaining positive relationships can be an important part of adjusting to life outside of prison. Stay connected with loved ones, and seek out support and guidance from trusted friends and family members. It can also be helpful to make an effort to reconnect with loved ones you may have lost touch with during your time in prison. Remember, you are not alone, and having a strong support network can be an important part of the reintegration process.

Adjusting to life outside of prison is a process, and it may take time. Be patient with yourself, and don't be afraid to seek out support and resources when you need them. You are not alone in this journey, and there are people and resources available to help

you succeed. Remember, you have the strength and resilience to
overcome the challenges of reintegration and build a better future for yourself.

Managing relationships: After being incarcerated, you may find that your relationships with loved ones have changed. It can be helpful to be open and honest with your loved ones about your experiences, and to work on rebuilding trust and communication.

Finding employment: Finding employment after incarceration can be challenging. Employers may be hesitant to hire someone with a criminal record, and you may have to overcome stigmas and biases. It can be helpful to seek out resources and programs that can help you find employment.

Managing finances: Managing finances after incarceration can be difficult, especially if you have limited resources or a criminal record that makes it harder to find employment. It can be helpful to create a budget, seek out financial assistance, and work on building your financial skills.

Coping with stigma: After being incarcerated, you may face stigma and discrimination from society. It can be helpful to seek out support from loved ones and from community resources, and to work on building your self-esteem and self-worth.

Understanding the challenges of reintegration is an important part of the process. By being aware of the challenges you may face, and by seeking out resources and support, you can work towards overcoming these challenges and building a better future for yourself.
Remember, you are not alone in this journey, and there are people and resources available to help you succeed. Don't be afraid to reach out for support when you need it.

CHAPTER 1 REVIEW NOTES

1) _______________________________________

____

____

2) _______________________________________

____

____

3) _______________________________________

____

____

4) _______________________________________

____

____

5) _______________________________________

____

____

6) _______________________________________

____

____

7) _______________________________________

____

____

8) _______________________________________

____

____

9) _______________________________________

____

10)

11)

12)

13)

14)

15)

16)

17)

18)

19)

20)

Chapter 2: Building a Support System after Incarceration

One of the key factors in successful reintegration after incarceration is having a strong support system in place. A support system can provide you with the emotional, practical, and financial support you need to overcome the challenges of reintegration and build a better future for yourself. In this chapter, we will discuss the importance of building a support system, and provide tips and strategies for doing so.

Seek out support from loved ones: Loved ones can be an important source of support as you reintegrate into society. This may include friends, family members, or romantic partners. It is important to be open and honest with your loved ones about your experiences and your needs, and to work on rebuilding trust and communication. Don't be afraid to ask for help when you need it, and remember that you are not alone in this journey.

Join a support group: Support groups can be a great resource for those who are reintegrating into society. These groups can provide a sense of community and support, and can help you connect with others who have gone through similar experiences. There are many different types of support groups available, so be sure to research and find one that is right for you.

Connect with community resources: There are many community resources available that can help you as you reintegrate into society. This may include social service agencies, faith-based organizations, or local non-profits. These resources can provide you with practical assistance, such as help with housing, employment, or financial needs, as well as emotional support.

Build a network of professional support: Building a network of professionals, such as a therapist, a job coach, or a financial advisor, can be helpful as you navigate the challenges of reintegration. These professionals can provide you with specialized support and guidance, and can help you build the skills and resources you need to succeed.

Remember, building a strong support system is an important part of the reintegration process. Don't be afraid to seek out support and to ask for help when you need it. You are not alone, and there are many people and resources available to help you succeed.

Consider joining a mentorship program: Mentorship programs can be a great way to connect with someone who has gone through similar experiences and can offer guidance and support as you reintegrate into society. These programs can provide you with a mentor who can offer advice, help you develop new skills, and provide emotional support. By working with a mentor, you can gain valuable insights and guidance that can help you navigate the challenges of reintegration.

Build your own support system: In addition to seeking out support from others, it is also important to build your own support system. This may include finding activities or hobbies that bring you joy, setting healthy boundaries with others, and taking care of your physical and mental health. Engaging in activities that nourish your body, mind, and spirit can help you feel more grounded and in control of your life. It can also be helpful to set aside time for relaxation and self-care, such as exercise, meditation, or taking a leisurely walk.

Be open to change: Building a support system may require you to make changes in your life. This may include letting go of negative relationships or seeking out new friends and communities. It is important to be open to these changes and to recognize that they can be an important part of the reintegration process. While it may be difficult to let go of familiar patterns and routines, embracing change can lead to new opportunities and a stronger support system.

Don't be afraid to ask for help: Reintegrating into society can be a challenging process, and it is important to remember that it is okay to ask for help. Don't be afraid to reach out to others for support, and don't be afraid to seek out resources and services that can help you. Whether it's seeking guidance from a therapist, joining a support group, or seeking out community resources, there are many people and organizations that can provide you with the support you need. Remember, you are not alone, and there are many people and resources available to help you succeed.

CHAPTER 2 REVIEW NOTES

1) _______________________________________

2) _______________________________________

3) _______________________________________

4) _______________________________________

5) _______________________________________

6) _______________________________________

7) _______________________________________

8) _______________________________________

9) _______________________________________

10) _______________________________

11) _______________________________

12) _______________________________

13) _______________________________

14) _______________________________

15) _______________________________

16) _______________________________

17) _______________________________

18) _______________________________

19) _______________________________

20) _______________________________

Chapter 3: Managing Finances and Finding Employment

One of the key challenges of reintegration after incarceration is finding and maintaining employment. In order to successfully reintegrate into society, it is important to have a stable source of income and to be able to manage your finances effectively. In this chapter, we will discuss strategies for finding employment and managing your finances as you reintegrate into society.

Start by assessing your skills and experience: Before you begin your job search, it is important to take inventory of your skills and experience. This may include any formal education or training you have received, as well as any work experience you have. Make a list of your skills and consider how they might be transferable to different industries or job roles.

Create a resume and cover letter: A well-written resume and cover letter can help you stand out to potential employers. Be sure to highlight your skills and experience, and consider including any training or education you have received. If you have gaps in your work history due to incarceration, consider explaining this in a cover letter or in an interview.

Network and seek out job leads: Networking can be a powerful tool in your job search. Connect with friends, family, and former colleagues, and consider joining professional organizations or job seeker groups. These connections can help you learn about job openings and may be able to provide you with leads or introductions.

Be prepared for job interviews: Job interviews can be intimidating, but they are an important part of the job search process. Be sure to research the company and the position you are applying for, and come prepared with specific examples of your skills and experience. Practice your interview skills with a friend or a mentor, and don't be afraid to ask for help if you need it.

Manage your finances: Once you have secured employment, it is important to manage your finances effectively. This may include setting a budget, creating a savings plan, and paying your bills on time. Consider seeking out financial education resources, such as a financial planner or a financial literacy program, to help you build strong financial habits.

Consider seeking out financial literacy trainings or programs: There are many financial literacy programs and resources available that can help you develop the skills and knowledge you need to manage your finances effectively. These programs may cover topics such as budgeting, saving, credit management, and financial planning. Financial literacy programs can be a valuable resource for those who are reintegrating into society, as they can provide you with the tools and knowledge you need to make informed financial decisions. Many organizations, such as non-profits, banks, and community centers, offer financial literacy programs, so be sure to research your options and find a program that is right for you.

Take advantage of financial resources and benefits: There may be financial resources and benefits available to you as you reintegrate into society. These may include government assistance programs, employer benefits, or financial resources offered by non-profit organizations. It is important to research your options and to be proactive in seeking out financial resources that can help you as you reintegrate into society. Don't be afraid to ask for help or to advocate for yourself when seeking out financial resources. There are many people and organizations that are willing to help, and it is important to take advantage of the resources that are available to you.

Build an emergency savings fund: One of the most important financial strategies you can implement is building an emergency savings fund. This fund should be used to cover unexpected expenses, such as car repairs or medical bills. By setting aside a small amount of money each month, you can build a financial safety net that can help you navigate unexpected challenges. Building an emergency savings fund can provide you with a sense of financial security and can help you feel more in control of your finances.

Don't be afraid to ask for help: If you are struggling to manage your finances or to find employment, don't be afraid to ask for help. There are many resources and organizations available that can provide you with financial guidance and support. This may include financial advisors, non-profit organizations, or government agencies. Don't be afraid to reach out and seek out the help you need. Remember, you are not alone, and there are many people and resources available to help you succeed.

Remember, finding and maintaining employment is an important part of the reintegration process. With determination and persistence, you can build a stable career and financial foundation as you reintegrate into society.

CHAPTER 3 REVIEW NOTES

1) ________________________________

2) ________________________________

3) ________________________________

4) ________________________________

5) ________________________________

6) ________________________________

7) ________________________________

8) ________________________________

9) ________________________________

10) ________________________________

11) ________________________________

12) _______________________________

13) _______________________________

14) _______________________________

15) _______________________________

16) _______________________________

17) _______________________________

18) _______________________________

19) _______________________________

20) _______________________________

Chapter 4: Navigating the Legal System

If you have been recently released from prison, you may be facing legal challenges as you reintegrate into society. It is important to understand your rights and responsibilities under the law, and to know how to navigate the legal system effectively. In this chapter, we will discuss strategies for navigating the legal system as you reintegrate into society.

Know your rights: It is important to understand your rights under the law, and to know how to assert them when necessary. This may include knowing your rights during a police encounter, or understanding your rights in the workplace.

Seek out legal resources: If you are facing legal challenges or have questions about the law, it is important to seek out legal resources. This may include consulting with a lawyer, or accessing legal resources through a non-profit organization or community center.

Understand the terms of your parole or probation: If you are on parole or probation, it is important to understand the terms of your release. This may include reporting requirements, restrictions on your activities or travel, or requirements to attend therapy or rehabilitation. It is important to follow the terms of your parole or probation to avoid any legal issues.

Learn about reentry laws and policies: There may be laws and policies in place that impact your reintegration into society. This may include laws related to employment, housing, or voting. It is important to understand these laws and policies, and to know how they may impact you as you reintegrate into society.

Don't be afraid to ask for help: If you are facing legal challenges or have questions about the law, don't be afraid to ask for help. There are many resources and organizations available that can provide you with legal guidance and support. This may include consulting with a lawyer, or accessing legal resources through a non-profit organization or community center. Remember, you are not alone, and there are many people and resources available to help you navigate the legal system effectively.

Stay informed: It is important to stay informed about changes in the law and how they may impact you. This may include keeping up with news and updates related to reentry laws and policies, or staying informed about developments in your particular legal case.

Know your options: If you are facing legal challenges, it is important to understand your options. This may include negotiating a plea deal, participating in a diversion program, or going to trial. It is important to understand the potential consequences and outcomes of each option, and to make informed decisions based on your individual circumstances.

Consider seeking out legal representation: If you are facing a serious legal issue, it may be in your best interest to seek out legal representation. A lawyer can provide you with legal counsel, represent you in court, and advocate on your behalf. While hiring a lawyer can be expensive, there are many resources available that can help you access legal representation, such as legal aid organizations or pro bono programs.

Stay on track: If you are on parole or probation, it is important to stay on track and follow the terms of your release. This may include meeting reporting requirements, attending therapy or rehabilitation, and avoiding any legal issues. By staying on track and following the terms of your parole or probation, you can successfully reintegrate into society and avoid any legal setbacks.

CHAPTER 4 REVIEW NOTES

1) ____

2) ____

3) ____

4) ____

5) ____

6) ____

7) ____

8) ____

9) ____

10) ____

11) ____

Chapter 5: Addressing Mental Health and Substance Abuse

For many people who have been recently released from prison, addressing mental health and substance abuse issues is a key part of the reintegration process. It is important to seek out resources and support to help you manage these issues and to build a healthy and stable foundation as you reintegrate into society. In this chapter, we will discuss strategies for addressing mental health and substance abuse as you reintegrate into society.

Seek out mental health resources: If you are experiencing mental health issues, it is important to seek out resources and support to help you manage your symptoms. This may include therapy, medication, or support groups. Many mental health resources are available, including through non-profit organizations, community centers, and government agencies.

Consider seeking out substance abuse treatment: If you are struggling with substance abuse issues, it is important to seek out treatment to help you manage your addiction. This may include inpatient or outpatient treatment, therapy, or support groups. Many substance abuse treatment resources are available, including through non-profit organizations, community centers, and government agencies.

Build a support network: Building a strong support network can be an important part of addressing mental health and substance abuse issues. This may include friends, family, and support groups who can provide you with emotional and practical support. It is important to surround yourself with people who are supportive and understanding, and who can help you navigate the challenges of reintegration.

Practice self-care: Taking care of your physical and emotional health is an important part of managing mental health and substance abuse issues. This may include engaging in activities that promote relaxation and stress management, such as exercise, meditation, or hobbies. It is important to find healthy ways to cope with stress and to prioritize your own well-being as you reintegrate into society.

Don't be afraid to ask for help: If you are struggling with mental health or substance abuse issues, don't be afraid to ask for help. There are many resources and organizations available that can provide you with support and guidance. This may include therapy, support groups, or non-profit organizations. Remember, you are not alone, and there are many people and resources available to help you succeed.

Take advantage of resources and benefits: There may be resources and benefits available to you as you address mental health and substance abuse issues. This may include government assistance programs, employer benefits, or financial resources offered by non-profit organizations. It is important to research your options and to be proactive in seeking out resources that can help you as you reintegrate into society.

Stay connected with your treatment team: If you are participating in therapy or substance abuse treatment, it is important to stay connected with your treatment team. This may include attending appointments, following through with treatment recommendations, and communicating openly with your therapist or treatment provider. By staying connected with your treatment team, you can get the support you need to manage your mental health and substance abuse issues.

Stay on track: It is important to stay on track and to follow through with your treatment plan as you address mental health and substance abuse issues. This may include taking medication as prescribed, attending therapy sessions, and participating in support groups. By staying on track, you can make progress in managing your mental health and substance abuse issues and build a stable foundation as you reintegrate into society.

Be patient: Addressing mental health and substance abuse issues can be a challenging process, and it is important to be patient with yourself as you work towards recovery. It may take time to make progress, and there may be setbacks along the way. It is important to be kind to yourself and to remember that progress is often made in small steps.

Consider seeking out treatment for PTSD: If you have experienced trauma or have symptoms of post-traumatic stress disorder (PTSD), it is important to seek out treatment. PTSD can affect your mental health and well-being, and it is important to get the help you need to manage your symptoms. Treatment options for PTSD may include therapy, medication, or a combination of both. Many resources are available for those who are struggling with PTSD, including through non-profit organizations, community centers, and government agencies.

Find healthy ways to cope with symptoms: If you are struggling with PTSD, it is important to find healthy ways to cope with your symptoms. This may include engaging in activities that promote relaxation and stress management, such as exercise, meditation, or hobbies. It is also important to find ways to process your thoughts and feelings about your trauma, such as through therapy or writing in a journal.

Build a support network: Building a strong support network can be an important part of managing PTSD. This may include friends, family, and support groups who can provide you with emotional and practical support. It is important to surround yourself with people who are supportive and understanding, and who can help you navigate the challenges of managing PTSD.

Don't be afraid to ask for help: If you are struggling with PTSD, don't be afraid to ask for help. There are many resources and organizations available that can provide you with support and guidance. This may include therapy, support groups, or non-profit organizations. Remember, you are not alone, and there are many people and resources available to help you succeed.

CHAPTER 5 REVIEW NOTES

1) _______________________________

2) _______________________________

3) _______________________________

4) _______________________________

5) _______________________________

6) _______________________________

7) _______________________________

8) _______________________________

9) _______________________________

10) _______________________________

11) _______________________________

Chapter 6

Practice Self-Care after Incarceration

Self-care is an important part of the reintegration process, and it is crucial to prioritize your own well-being as you adjust to life outside of prison. Taking care of your physical and emotional health can help you build a stable foundation and navigate the challenges of reintegration more effectively. In this chapter, we will discuss strategies for practicing self-care as you reintegrate into society.

Make time for self-care: It is important to make time for self-care, even if you have a busy schedule. This may include setting aside time for activities that promote relaxation and stress management, such as exercise, meditation, or hobbies. It is important to prioritize self-care, and to make it a regular part of your routine.

Seek out support: Building a strong support network can be an important part of practicing self-care. This may include friends, family, or support groups who can provide you with emotional and practical support. It is important to surround yourself with people who are supportive and understanding, and who can help you navigate the challenges of reintegration.

Engage in healthy behaviors: Practicing self-care also involves engaging in healthy behaviors that promote physical and emotional well-being. This may include eating a healthy diet, getting enough sleep, and engaging in regular physical activity. It is important to prioritize healthy habits as you reintegrate into society.

Seek out mental health resources: If you are experiencing mental health issues, it is important to seek out resources and support to help you manage your symptoms. This may include therapy, medication, or support groups. Many mental health resources are available, including through non-profit organizations, community centers, and government agencies.

Don't be afraid to ask for help: If you are struggling with self-care or have concerns about your mental health, don't be afraid to ask for help. There are many resources and organizations available that can provide you with support and guidance. This may include therapy, support groups, or non-profit organizations. Remember, you are not alone, and there are many people and resources available to help you succeed.

Practice mindfulness: Engaging in mindfulness practices, such as meditation or yoga, can be an effective way to reduce stress and improve well-being. These practices can help you to become more present and focused, and can promote relaxation and calmness. There are many resources available to help you learn mindfulness techniques, including through non-profit organizations, community centers, and online resources.

Seek out self-care resources: There are many resources available to help you practice self-care after incarceration. This may include non-profit organizations, community centers, and online resources that offer activities and services to promote relaxation and well-being. It is important to research your options and to seek out resources that can support your self-care goals.

Take breaks: It is important to take breaks and to give yourself time to rest and recharge. This may involve setting aside time for relaxation, or engaging in activities that promote relaxation, such as taking a walk or listening to music. It is important to listen to your body and to take breaks when you need them.

Set boundaries: Setting boundaries is an important part of self-care, and it involves setting limits on the amount of time and energy you spend on activities and relationships. This may involve saying no to requests or commitments that are not aligned with your goals or values, or setting limits on your interactions with others. Setting boundaries can help you to prioritize your own well-being and to manage your time and energy effectively.

CHAPTER 6 REVIEW NOTES

1) ____

____

2) ____

____

3) ____

____

4) ____

____

5) ____

____

6) ____

____

7) ____

____

8) ____

____

9) ____

____

10) ____

____

11) ____

____

____

Chapter 7

Building and Maintaining Positive Relationships

Building and maintaining positive relationships is an important part of the reintegration process. Connecting with others can provide you with emotional and practical support, and can help you navigate the challenges of reintegration more effectively. In this chapter, we will discuss strategies for building and maintaining positive relationships as you reintegrate into society.

Seek out positive relationships: Building positive relationships is an important part of the reintegration process, and it involves connecting with others who are supportive and understanding. This may include friends, family, or support groups who can provide you with emotional and practical support. It is important to surround yourself with people who are positive and supportive, and who can help you navigate the challenges of reintegration.

Communicate openly and honestly: Building and maintaining positive relationships involves being open and honest with others. This may include sharing your thoughts, feelings, and needs, and being willing to listen to the perspectives of others. By communicating openly and honestly, you can build trust and strengthen your relationships.

Practice empathy: Empathy involves understanding and being sensitive to the feelings of others. Practicing empathy can help you to build and maintain positive relationships, and it involves being understanding and compassionate towards others. By showing empathy, you can create a sense of connection and build trust in your relationships.

Set boundaries: Setting boundaries is an important part of building and maintaining positive relationships. This involves setting limits on the amount of time and energy you spend on activities and relationships, and being clear about your needs and expectations. Setting boundaries can help you to maintain healthy and positive relationships, and to manage your time and energy effectively.

Seek out relationship resources: There are many resources available to help you build and maintain positive relationships after incarceration. This may include therapy, support groups, or non-profit organizations that offer relationship education and support. It is important to research your options and to seek out resources that can support your relationship goals.

Practice forgiveness: Forgiveness is an important part of building and maintaining positive relationships, and it involves letting go of resentment or anger towards others. Practice forgiveness as a way to move past conflicts and to build stronger and more positive relationships.

Seek out conflict resolution resources: If you are struggling with conflicts in your relationships, it is important to seek out resources to help you resolve these issues. This may include therapy, support groups, or non-profit organizations that offer conflict resolution education and support. By addressing conflicts in a healthy and constructive way, you can build stronger and more positive relationships.

Focus on the present: Building and maintaining positive relationships involves being present and engaged in your interactions with others. This means being fully present in the moment, rather than dwelling on the past or worrying about the future. By focusing on the present, you can build stronger and more positive relationships.

Foster a sense of connection: Building positive relationships involves fostering a sense of connection and shared experience with others. This may involve engaging in activities or hobbies that you enjoy together, or spending time talking and listening to each other. By fostering a sense of connection, you can build stronger and more positive relationships.

CHAPTER 7 REVIEW

1)

2)

3)

4)

5)

6)

7)

8)

9)

10)

Chapter 8

Creating a Plan for the Future

Creating a plan for the future is an important part of the reintegration process, and it involves setting goals and taking steps towards achieving them. By creating a plan, you can focus your efforts and resources on the things that are most important to you, and increase your chances of success. In this chapter, we will discuss strategies for creating a plan for the future as you reintegrate into society.

Identify your values and goals: The first step in creating a plan for the future is to identify your values and goals. What is most important to you, and what do you hope to achieve in your life? By identifying your values and goals, you can create a roadmap for your future and focus your efforts on the things that matter most to you.

Create SMART goals: SMART goals are specific, measurable, achievable, relevant, and time-bound. Creating SMART goals can help you to focus your efforts and increase your chances of success. When creating your goals, be sure to make them specific, measurable, achievable, relevant, and time-bound.

SMART goals are a framework for setting and achieving goals. The acronym SMART stands for Specific, Measurable, Achievable, Relevant, and Time-bound. Using this framework can help you to create clear, actionable goals that are more likely to be achieved.

Specific: Specific goals are clear and well-defined, and they focus on a specific outcome. For example, "I want to save $5,000 for a down payment on a house" is a specific goal. Specific goals are easier to focus on and to take action towards.

Measurable: Measurable goals are quantifiable and have clear benchmarks for progress. For example, "I want to save $500 per month for the next 10 months" is a measurable goal. By measuring your progress, you can track your progress and stay motivated.

Achievable: Achievable goals are realistic and within your reach. It is important to set goals that are challenging, but not impossible. For example, "I want to save $500 per month for the next 10 months" is an achievable goal if you have the resources and plan in place to reach it.

Relevant: Relevant goals are aligned with your values and priorities, and they are meaningful to you. For example, "I want to save $5,000 for a down payment on a house" is a relevant goal if owning a home is important to you. Relevant goals are more motivating and rewarding to work towards.

Time-bound: Time-bound goals have a specific timeline for completion. This helps to give your goals a sense of urgency and helps you to stay focused and motivated. For example, "I want to save $500 per month for the next 10 months" is a time-bound goal. By setting a deadline, you can stay on track and make progress towards your goal.

Break your goals down into smaller steps: Once you have identified your goals, it is important to break them down into smaller steps. This can help you to focus your efforts and make progress towards your goals. By breaking your goals down into smaller steps, you can create a plan of action and track your progress over time.

Seek out resources and support: There are many resources available to help you create and achieve your goals. This may include therapy, support groups, or non-profit organizations that offer goal setting and achievement support. It is important to research your options and to seek out resources that can support your goals.

Be flexible and adaptable: Creating a plan for the future involves being flexible and adaptable. Things may not always go as planned, and it is important to be open to change and to adapt to new situations. By being flexible and adaptable, you can adjust your plan as needed and stay on track towards achieving your goals.

Review and revise your plan: It is important to review and revise your plan regularly to ensure that it is still relevant and aligned with your values and goals. This may involve reassessing your goals, identifying new steps or resources, or making adjustments as needed. By reviewing and revising your plan, you can ensure that you are making progress towards your goals and that your plan is still aligned with your values and priorities.

Seek out support and accountability: Building a strong support network and seeking out accountability can be an important part of creating and achieving your goals. This may involve sharing your goals with friends, family, or support groups, and seeking out feedback and guidance as you work towards your objectives. By seeking out support and accountability, you can increase your chances of success and stay motivated and on track.

Stay motivated and focused: Achieving your goals requires motivation and focus. It is important to keep your goals in mind and to stay focused on your progress. There will be setbacks and challenges along the way, and it is important to stay motivated and committed to your goals. By staying motivated and focused, you can increase your chances of success.

Celebrate your achievements: Achieving your goals is a cause for celebration, and it is important to take time to celebrate your achievements along the way. This may involve acknowledging your progress, reflecting on your accomplishments, or sharing your success with others. By celebrating your achievements, you can stay motivated and focused on your goals.

CHAPTER 8 REVIEW NOTES

1) _______________________________________

____

2) _______________________________________

____

3) _______________________________________

____

4) _______________________________________

____

5) _______________________________________

____

6) _______________________________________

____

7) _______________________________________

____

8) _______________________________________

____

9) _______________________________________

____

10) _______________________________________

____

11) _______________________________________

____

____

Chapter 9

Finding Housing and Building a Home

Finding housing and building a home is an important part of the reintegration process, and it involves finding a place to live that is safe, affordable, and suitable for your needs. In this chapter, we will discuss strategies for finding housing and building a home as you reintegrate into society.

Research your options: There are many options for finding housing, and it is important to research your options to find the best fit for your needs. This may include looking at apartments, houses, or shared living arrangements, and considering factors such as location, price, and amenities. It is also important to consider any special needs or requirements you may have, such as accessibility or support services.

Develop a budget: Creating a budget is an important part of finding housing and building a home, and it involves identifying your income and expenses and determining how much you can afford to spend on housing. It is important to be realistic and to consider other expenses you may have, such as utilities, transportation, and food. By developing a budget, you can ensure that you are able to afford your housing and other necessities.

Seek out financial resources: There are many financial resources available to help you find housing and build a home, including government assistance programs, non-profit organizations, and financial institutions. It is important to research your options and to seek out resources that can help you to meet your housing needs.

Consider your support network: Building a home involves more than just finding a place to live – it also involves building a support network of friends, family, and community resources. It is important to consider the support you have available when choosing your housing, and to identify any additional resources you may need.

Take care of your home: Building a home involves taking care of your living space and maintaining it in a clean and safe condition. This may involve regular cleaning and maintenance, paying bills and rent on time, and being respectful of your neighbors. By taking care of your home, you can create a comfortable and welcoming living space.

CHAPTER 9 REVIEW NOTES

1)

2)

3)

4)

5)

6)

7)

8)

9)

10)

11)

Chapter 10

Connecting with Community Resources

Connecting with community resources is an important part of the reintegration process, and it involves finding and accessing the services and support that are available in your community. In this chapter, we will discuss strategies for connecting with community resources as you reintegrate into society.

Research your options: There are many community resources available, and it is important to research your options to find the services and support that are most suitable for your needs. This may include looking for resources online, reaching out to local non-profit organizations, or contacting your local government or community center.

Seek out referrals and recommendations: Asking for referrals and recommendations from friends, family, or other trusted sources can be a helpful way to connect with community resources. These recommendations can provide valuable insights and help you to find the resources that are most suitable for your needs.

Consider your needs and goals: When connecting with community resources, it is important to consider your needs and goals. What services or support do you need, and how can community resources help you to achieve your goals? By identifying your needs and goals, you can better match your needs with the resources that are available.

Be proactive: Connecting with community resources often involves being proactive and taking the initiative to seek out the resources you need. This may involve making phone calls, filling out applications, or attending events or workshops. By being proactive, you can increase your chances of finding the resources you need.

Utilize online resources: Many community resources are now available online, which can make it easier to connect with the support and services you need. This may include websites, social media groups, or online directories of resources. By utilizing online resources, you can find the support you need more quickly and easily.

Join support groups: Support groups can be an excellent way to connect with others who have similar experiences or challenges, and they can provide valuable support, resources, and encouragement. Many communities offer support groups for a variety of issues, such as addiction, mental health, parenting, and more.

Consider transportation: Accessing community resources may require transportation, and it is important to consider this when connecting with resources. If you do not have a car, you may need to rely on public transportation, ride-sharing services, or other options. It is important to consider your transportation needs and to plan accordingly.

Don't be afraid to ask for help: Connecting with community resources often involves seeking out help and support, and it is important to not be afraid to ask for help when you need it. Many people are willing to offer assistance and support, and by asking for help, you can access the resources you need to thrive in your community.

Stay open to new opportunities: Connecting with community resources involves staying open to new opportunities and being willing to try new things. You may discover new resources or services that can be beneficial to you, and by staying open to new opportunities, you can continue to grow and thrive in your community.

Stay engaged and connected: Connecting with community resources is an ongoing process, and it is important to stay engaged and connected to the resources and support that are available. This may involve attending events, joining groups or organizations, or staying informed about new resources and services. By staying engaged and connected, you can continue to access the resources you need to thrive in your community.

CHAPTER 10 REVIEW NOTES

1) ____

2) ____

3) ____

4) ____

5) ____

6) ____

7) ____

8) ____

9) ____

10) ____

11) ____

Chapter 11

Managing Stress and Coping with Setbacks

Managing stress and coping with setbacks is an important part of the reintegration process, and it involves finding healthy ways to handle the challenges and stresses you may encounter as you transition back into society. In this chapter, we will discuss strategies for managing stress and coping with setbacks as you reintegrate into society.

Identify your stressors: The first step in managing stress is to identify the sources of stress in your life. What are the things that cause you stress, and how do they affect you? By identifying your stressors, you can better understand what is causing your stress and how to address it.

Develop healthy coping strategies: There are many healthy coping strategies that can help you to manage stress and cope with setbacks. This may include activities such as exercise, meditation, or spending time with friends and loved ones. It is important to find the coping strategies that work best for you and to incorporate them into your daily routine.

Seek out support: Building a strong support network can be an important part of managing stress and coping with setbacks. This may involve seeking out friends, family, or professionals who can offer support and guidance. By seeking out support, you can find the help you need to cope with challenges and setbacks.

Practice self-care: Taking care of yourself is an important part of managing stress and coping with setbacks. This may involve getting enough rest, eating a healthy diet, and engaging in activities that bring you joy and relaxation. By practicing self-care, you can improve your overall well-being and better manage stress.

Learn stress management techniques: There are many techniques that can help you to manage stress and cope with setbacks, including relaxation techniques such as deep breathing, progressive muscle relaxation, or guided imagery. It is important to learn these techniques and to practice them regularly in order to better manage stress and cope with challenges.

Set realistic goals: Setting realistic goals can be an important part of managing stress and coping with setbacks. By setting achievable goals, you can feel a sense of accomplishment and progress, which can help you to feel more in control of your life.

Take breaks and practice self-compassion: It is important to take breaks and to be kind to yourself when you are facing stress or setbacks. This may involve taking time to rest, engaging in activities that bring you joy, or seeking out support from friends and loved ones. By practicing self-compassion, you can better cope with challenges and setbacks.

Manage your time effectively: Time management can be an important part of managing stress and coping with setbacks. By prioritizing your tasks and being mindful of how you spend your time, you can reduce stress and better manage your responsibilities.

Seek out positive influences: Surrounding yourself with positive influences can be an important part of managing stress and coping with setbacks. This may involve seeking out friends and loved ones who are supportive and uplifting, or engaging in activities that bring you joy and positivity. By seeking out positive influences, you can better manage stress and cope with challenges.

Seek professional help: If you are struggling to cope with stress or setbacks, it may be helpful to seek out professional help. This may involve talking to a therapist, counselor, or other mental health professional who can offer guidance and support. By seeking professional help, you can get the support you need to manage stress and cope with challenges.

CHAPTER 11 REVIEW NOTES

1)

2)

3)

4)

5)

6)

7)

8)

9)

10)

11)

Chapter 12

Building a Strong Support Network

Building a strong support network is an important part of the reintegration process, and it involves finding and connecting with individuals and groups who can offer you support and guidance as you transition back into society. In this chapter, we will discuss strategies for building a strong support network as you reintegrate into society.

Identify your support needs: The first step in building a strong support network is to identify your support needs. What kinds of support do you need, and who can offer it to you? By identifying your support needs, you can better understand what you are looking for in a support network.

Seek out friends and loved ones: Friends and loved ones can be an important part of your support network, and it is important to reach out to them for support and guidance. This may involve spending time with them, talking about your challenges and goals, or simply seeking out their presence and support.

Join groups or organizations: Groups and organizations can be an excellent way to connect with others who have similar experiences or challenges, and they can provide valuable support and resources. Many communities offer groups and organizations for a variety of issues, such as addiction, mental health, parenting, and more.

Consider professional support: Professional support can be an important part of your support network, and it may involve seeking out therapists, counselors, or other mental health professionals. These professionals can offer guidance and support as you navigate the challenges of reintegration.

Utilize online resources: Many community resources are now available online, which can make it easier to connect with the support and services you need. This may include websites, social media groups, or online directories of resources. By utilizing online resources, you can find the support you need more quickly and easily.

Volunteer: Volunteering can be an excellent way to connect with others and to give back to your community. By volunteering, you can not only help others, but you can also build relationships and find a sense of purpose and meaning.

Attend support groups: Support groups can be an excellent way to connect with others who have similar experiences or challenges, and they can provide valuable support, resources, and encouragement. Many communities offer support groups for a variety of issues, such as addiction, mental health, parenting, and more.

Consider seeking support from faith-based organizations: If you have a spiritual or religious practice, you may find it helpful to seek support from faith-based organizations. These organizations can provide a sense of community and connection, and they may offer resources and support that can be beneficial to you.

Don't be afraid to ask for help: Building a strong support network often involves seeking out help and support, and it is important to not be afraid to ask for help when you need it. Many people are willing to offer assistance and support, and by asking for help, you can access the resources you need to thrive in your community.

Stay connected: Building and maintaining a strong support network is an ongoing process, and it is important to stay connected to the people and resources that offer you support. This may involve staying in touch with friends and loved ones, attending events or meetings, or staying informed about new resources and services. By staying connected, you can continue to access the support you need to thrive in your community.

CHAPTER 12 REVIEW NOTES

1) _______________________________

2) _______________________________

3) _______________________________

4) _______________________________

5) _______________________________

6) _______________________________

7) _______________________________

8) _______________________________

9) _______________________________

10) _______________________________

11) _______________________________

SUMMARY

This book is a comprehensive guide to the challenges and opportunities of reintegration into society for formerly incarcerated individuals and their families. It provides valuable information, resources, and support for navigating the reintegration process and building a fulfilling and successful life after prison.

The chapters in this book cover a wide range of topics that are important for the reintegration process, including understanding the challenges of reintegration, building a strong support network, managing finances and finding employment, navigating the legal system, addressing mental health and substance abuse, practicing self-care, building and maintaining positive relationships, creating a plan for the future, finding housing and building a home, and connecting with community resources.

This book is written in a friendly and supportive tone, and it is designed to provide practical guidance and support to those who are facing the challenges of reintegration. It is our hope that this book will serve as a valuable resource for all who read it, and that it will empower and support those who are working to build a better future for themselves and their communities.

Department of Rehabilitation (DOR) program offers a variety of resources and services to help individuals achieve their goals and succeed in their endeavors. Some of the ways in which we may be able to assist include:

- Navigating and accessing disability and benefits programs.

- Providing job search and interview skills training.

- Offering job training and tools to help individuals develop new skills and succeed in their careers.

- Assisting with college expenses, including textbooks and other materials.

- Providing disability equipment to help individuals overcome physical challenges.

- Offering support services such as childcare and transportation to help individuals overcome logistical barriers.

Connecting individuals with other people or groups that may be able to provide additional support and resources.

Resources:

**Department of Rehabilitation
2323 W Manchester Blvd,
Inglewood, CA 90305
(323) 565-1860**

**Department of Rehabilitation
4300 Long Beach Blvd #200,
Long Beach, CA 90807
(562) 422-8325**

**Department of Rehabilitation
888 S Figueroa St Suite 900,
Los Angeles, CA 90017
(213) 736-3904**

**Department of Rehabilitation
15400 Sherman Way UNIT 140,
Van Nuys, CA 91406
(818) 901-5024**

Here are some national hotlines for depression in the United States:

- National Suicide Prevention Lifeline: 1-800-273-TALK (8255)
- Substance Abuse and Mental Health Services Administration (SAMHSA) National Helpline: 1-800-662-HELP (4357)
- National Alliance on Mental Illness (NAMI) Helpline: 1-800-950-NAMI (6264)

Here are some national hotlines for substance abuse in the United States:

- Substance Abuse and Mental Health Services Administration (SAMHSA) National Helpline: 1-800-662-HELP (4357)
- National Institute on Drug Abuse (NIDA) Hotline: 1-855-678-6232
- Alcohol and Drug Helpline: 1-800-821-4357
- Narcotics Anonymous: 1-877-669-1669

Here are some national hotlines for employment resources in the United States:

- Department of Labor Career One Stop: 1-877-348-0502
- National Resume Writers' Association: 1-800-845-0586
- Job Corps: 1-800-733-5627
- Veterans' Employment and Training Service: 1-800-424-8387

Here are some national hotlines for support groups in the United States:

- National Alliance on Mental Illness (NAMI) Helpline: 1-800-950-NAMI (6264)
- Alcoholics Anonymous: 1-212-870-3400
- Al-Anon/Alateen Hotline: 1-888-4AL-ANON (1-888-425-2666)
- National Eating Disorders Association Helpline: 1-800-931-2237
- The Trevor Project (LGBTQ+ support): 1-866-488-7386

Remember, you are not alone in your struggles and there is always hope for a better tomorrow. Take the first step towards a brighter future by reaching out for help and support.

You are capable of overcoming any obstacle and achieving your goals.
Don't hesitate to visit www.ucanla.org or email UCANINC5@gmail.com for more information on the resources and support available to you.

Together, we can make a positive change in your life and in the community. Believe in yourself and your abilities, and never give up on your dreams."

DeJuan L. Verrett

MAKING A DIFFERENCE!